AF527013

GEOGRAPHY ENCYCLOPEDIA

UNIVERSE AND EARTH

Om KIDZ
An imprint of Om Books International

CONTENTS

Inside the Universe	4
Starry Galaxies	6
Exploring the Solar System	8
Gigantic Gas Giants	10
Incredible Ice Giants	11
Other Celestial Bodies	12
Marvellous Moon	13
Understanding Eclipses	14
Home-made Satellites	16
Terrific Terrestrial Planets	17
Earth and its Neighbour	18
Continental Drift	20
The Plate Tectonics Theory	22
Continents: Asia and Africa	24
Continents: North America and South America	25
Continents: Antarctica, Europe and Australia	26
The Great Barrier Reef	28
Hot Springs and Geysers	30
Uluru and Kata Tjuta	31
Aurora Borealis and Aurora Australis	32

MYSTERIOUS UNIVERSE

All the planets of our solar system, including Earth, our galaxy and a million other galaxies are contained within the universe. The universe is the sum total of all matter and energy that exists. It is a "cosmos", which means that it has a complicated, but organised system.

It is proposed that our universe was once an extremely, dark, hot and heavy matter. We do not know much about what the matter was, where it came from and how it was formed. However, we know that it expanded and cooled over billions of years to form our universe. This theory is known as the "Big Bang".

A very popular (and untrue) myth states that the universe began with a giant, fiery explosion. This is why the theory was named the "Big Bang" theory. As a result, people often confuse the origin of the universe, thinking that it started with a big bang.

INSIDE THE UNIVERSE

We live on Earth and share it with approximately seven billion other people. We also share our Earth with animals, forests and large bodies of water. Our Earth, along with other planets and the Sun, is a part of the solar system. Our solar system is contained within the Milky Way galaxy.

There are 100 billion other galaxies like the Milky Way galaxy. Each galaxy, in turn, has billions of stars, several constellations, moons, asteroids and other heavenly bodies. All of these are called "celestial bodies", which make up the universe.

How big is the universe?

The universe is said to be infinite or never-ending. But, this has not been proven. No one knows if the universe has an end. There are parts of the universe that we know exist, but are yet to explore. There are also many parts of the universe of which we know nothing about and cannot even see, which means we cannot even explore them. So, we cannot measure or find out the size of the entire universe.

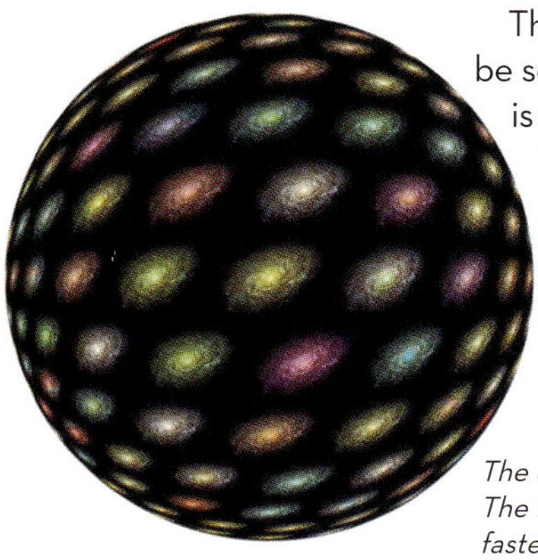

The area of the universe that can be seen and observed from Earth is called "observable universe". Imagine this observable universe to be elliptical in shape. Its diameter is said to be 91 billion light years. It is big enough to contain 100 billion galaxies.

The universe is an expanding sphere. The faraway galaxies are moving the fastest. As a result, they experience a shortening of length. So, they might seem smaller to an observer.

Light year

A light year is a unit of length. We use this unit to measure distances between things within the Milky Way, the distances between two separate stars or galaxies, and also the distances between other things in the universe.

Measuring space

Have you heard of the Astronomical Unit (AU)? It is a unit of length that is used to measure the distance between different planets or the distance between a planet and the Sun. The distance between Earth and the Sun is 1 AU.

The distances between planets and their moons are measured in kilometres or miles. One light year is the same as 9.5 trillion kms.

FUN FACT

You may not be able to see things that are very far away from you. This is because of time. This means that light has not reached the distance you cannot see because it did not have enough time to do so.

The observable universe

This photo shows the universe before many stars and galaxies were formed. This is why it is called the youngest photo of the universe. It is also called the oldest photo because light took about 13.8 billion years to reach us.

The observable universe is a sphere that has a diameter of 13.8 billion light years. Hence, a person trying to observe any part of the universe using a telescope can only see within a distance of 13.8 billion light years.

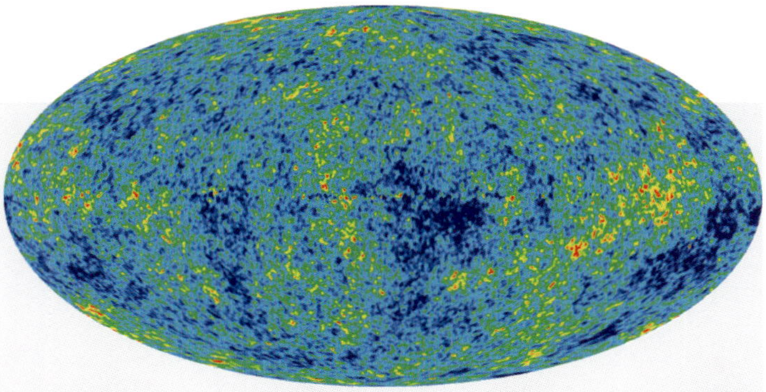

This photo is called the youngest and oldest photo of the universe.

What is the universe made of?

Scientists have been trying to understand exactly what the universe is made of. To understand how and why the universe evolved to what it is today, we need to know what it is made of. The universe is said to be made up of three different types of substances. However, this is still a topic of debate today. These substances are called "normal matter", "dark matter" and "dark energy".

Dark matter

Dark matter cannot be seen using a telescope. It has a large gravitational pull and greatly affects the mass or weight of things that are visible. Though this matter is invisible, scientists believe that 25 per cent of the universe is made up of dark matter.

A large portion of the universe is said to be made of dark energy. We do not know much about it. There are many contradictory opinions about dark energy. Many people believe that it is present throughout our infinite universe and is an important factor behind the continuous expansion of our universe. However, some believe that no such matter exists.

Artist's imagination of what dark matter looks like in space.

"Stuff of life"

Atoms are made up of protons, neutrons and electrons. They are called "normal matter" or "baryonic matter". Together, they are said to be "the stuff of life". Stars and all things found on Earth, including human beings, are made up of protons, neutrons and electrons. Hydrogen, helium, carbon, uranium and iron are a combination of these protons and neutrons. A few decades ago, it was incorrectly believed that the entire universe was made of normal matter. Now we know that only about 10 per cent of it makes up our universe.

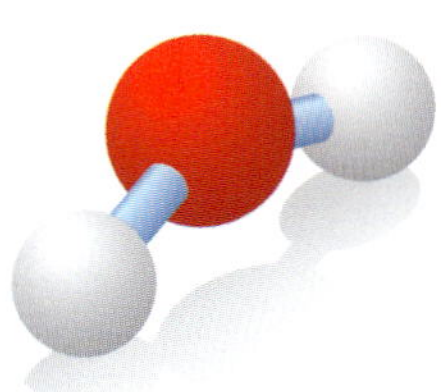

STARRY GALAXIES

A galaxy is a group or collection of billions of stars, gas clouds, dust and dark matter that exist together due to a strong gravitational force exerted upon them. Galaxies also have smaller clusters of stars.

The word "galaxy" comes from the Greek word *galaxias* meaning "milky". This also inspired the name of our home galaxy, the Milky Way. As we have not explored all parts of the universe, we do not know the exact number of galaxies that exist in the universe.

Star clusters

A star cluster is a group of stars that are bound together by a strong gravitational force. A star cluster can be big or small and can form different shapes. It could have many stars or a few stars. There are some star clusters that are a billion years old, while some are just thousands of years old.

Types of galaxies

After carefully studying and understanding the structure, shape and forms of different galaxies, astronomers have classified them as elliptical, spiral and irregular.

Do you want to see a galaxy?

Galaxies are very far away from us. But there are some galaxies that are so bright that we can see them from Earth without using a telescope or any special device. The Andromeda Galaxy, which is the closest galaxy to Earth, can be seen from Earth even on a dark, New Moon night!

Andromeda galaxy.

Elliptical galaxy

As the name suggests, an elliptical galaxy has an elliptical or egg-shaped appearance and can either be flat or slightly spherical. Very rarely do these galaxies form new stars as they lack the gases and dust clouds required to form them. So, they mainly contain older stars. Astronomers believe that every elliptical galaxy has a black hole at the centre and that this black hole makes up for most of its total mass.

An elliptical galaxy.

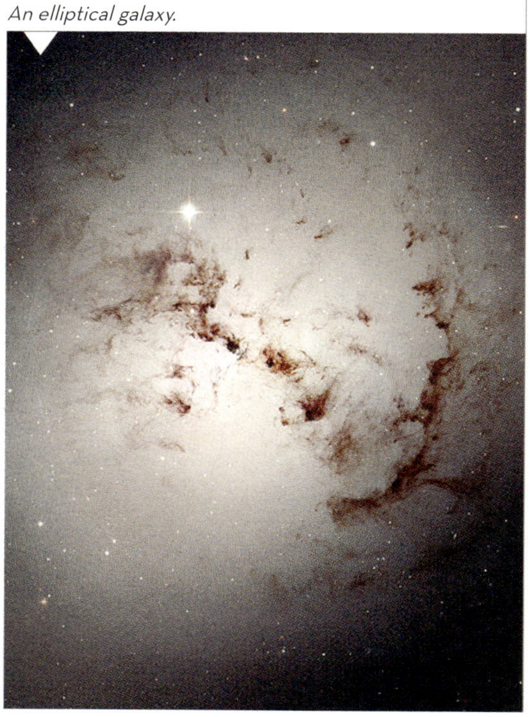

Spiral galaxy

Spiral galaxy is the more common type of galaxy found in the universe. It is flat and has a bulge at the centre or core known as the "galactic bulge", which is extremely bright as it consists of clusters of old stars. It has long arms that spiral away from this bulge. The arms form a flat, disc-like structure where new stars are formed. They also contain many young stars.

A spiral galaxy.

The Virgo Supercluster

A group of galaxies is termed as "a cluster of galaxies". About 40 galaxies together, including the Milky Way and Andromeda galaxy, form a galaxy cluster known as the "Local Group". About 65 million light years away is another cluster of galaxies known as the "Virgo Cluster". These clusters are contained within the Virgo Supercluster, which has a diameter of about 110 million light years.

Our very own Milky Way is contained within the Virgo Supercluster, which has around 100 other galaxies.

FUN FACT

From the image taken by the Chandra space telescope, scientists have been able to observe that the black hole at the centre of the Milky Way, named Sagittarius A* (read as Sagittarius A star), is 3 million times greater in size than our massive Sun!

An illustration of the Chandra X-ray Observatory holding the Chandra space telescope.

Barred spiral galaxy

Some spiral galaxies have a line or bar of stars and other matter running across their centres. They are further classified as barred spiral galaxies. The Milky Way galaxy is a barred spiral galaxy.

A barred spiral galaxy.

Irregular galaxy

Most galaxies have specific shape, however, the irregular galaxy, as its name suggests, has an irregular shape. Irregular galaxies may have started out as spiral galaxies. At one point, these galaxies possibly had close contact with, or travelled through, another galaxy, causing its shape to undergo a large alteration.

This interaction forces the formation of new stars. Therefore, irregular galaxies have a large number of very new or young stars.

An irregular galaxy.

The Milky Way

The Milky Way is home to our Earth and the rest of the solar system. It is flat and shaped like a disc. Earth is about 27,000 light years away from the core of the Milky Way. Using the Chandra space telescope, we have been able to get a view of the centre of our galaxy. Just like all barred spiral galaxies, it has many stars and star clusters at its centre.

The Milky Way galaxy.

EXPLORING THE SOLAR SYSTEM

Our Earth is a part of the solar system. Earth, the seven other planets, dwarf planets, asteroids, meteoroids, comets and satellites, both natural and artificial, make up the solar system. All of these celestial bodies move around the Sun in a systematic manner. The Sun is said to be at the heart of the solar system.

A hot, boiling star

The Sun is the largest object in the solar system. It accounts for nearly 99 per cent of the solar system's mass despite entirely being made up of two of the lightest gases in the universe—hydrogen and helium. The Sun provides energy, heat and light to Earth. Life cannot exist on Earth without the Sun and all that it provides us with.

The Sun is a star. Stars are entirely made up of gases. The Sun is also made up of about 92 per cent of hydrogen and 8 per cent of helium. Constant nuclear reactions occur at the core of the Sun. The hydrogen gas in the Sun's core is converted to helium. This is how all of the Sun's energy is produced.

An eruption at the surface of the Sun.

How hot is the Sun?

The Sun is extremely hot. From Earth, it appears to have a yellow or orange colour. This is because it has a surface temperature of 5,500 °C. As impressive as the Sun is, there are many other stars like the Sun in the Milky Way and in the universe that are possibly bigger, brighter and hotter! There are much larger stars in the entire universe.

Is the Sun at the exact centre?

No. While we say that the Sun is the centre of the solar system, remember that this does not mean an exact centre. It is not like the centre of a circle. However, its position is very near to the centre.

FUN FACT

The Pacific Ocean is the biggest ocean on Earth; Jupiter has the biggest ocean in the solar system!

The geocentric model

We have had to overcome several misconceptions to truly understand the solar system and build our knowledge to what it is today. It was earlier believed that Earth is the centre of the solar system and that the Sun moves around it. This belief was formed because, we can see that the Sun is at different positions during different times of the day. A long time ago, it was also believed that Earth is stationary. It does not change its position or move at all. This is known as the geocentric model of the solar system.

Why did people believe the geocentric model?

Aristotle supported the geocentric model and the theory that Earth is stationary. He said that we cannot feel the movement of the Earth because it does not move. He argued that the movement of Earth should create wind. He also said that clouds and birds would constantly need to keep up with Earth's movements because of the wind it would create.

"Earth is not a planet".

According to the geocentric model, Earth is not a planet, but a heavenly body at the very heart of our solar system. Also, according to this model, the moon and the Sun are to be considered planets along with Mercury, Venus, Mars, Jupiter and Saturn.

"Earthrise" was a photograph taken by astronauts with Earth as a celestial body.

There were some scholars who could not explain or understand this model. One such scholar was Aristarchus of Samos from Turkey. In 200 BCE, he was the very first thinker to put forth the idea that the Sun, and not Earth, could be at the centre of the solar system. This theory, however, was not accepted by the masses at first because it did not explain the many changing positions of the Sun and the moon.

The heliocentric model

During the sixteenth century, a renowned astronomer named Nicolaus Copernicus worked on Aristarchus' theory and built the heliocentric model. In this model, Earth orbits around the Sun along with the other planets. Copernicus positioned Earth behind Mercury and Venus, and said that the moon moves around Earth. He also explained that Earth itself rotates, which makes it seem like the Sun and the stars are moving.

Galileo and Johannes Kepler benefited from Copernicus' model and further developed the heliocentric model. They tried to find mathematical and scientific proof, and answered some of the doubts raised by their peers.

An illustration of the heliocentric model of the solar system.

GIGANTIC GAS GIANTS

Jupiter, Saturn, Uranus and Neptune are called outer planets. They are also called "gas giants" or "Jovian giants", because they are made up of large quantities of hydrogen and helium gases.

Jupiter

Saturn

Jupiter

Jupiter is the fifth planet from the Sun. It is the biggest planet in our solar system as its size is two and a half times greater than the other planets. It is more than 10 times greater than Earth. The Sun, Venus, moon and Jupiter (in that order) are the brightest bodies in our solar system. Jupiter takes 12 Earth years to complete one orbit around the Sun. A day in Jupiter only lasts for 9 hours and 55 minutes, which is the shortest duration for a day on any planet. It has 62 "known" moons; scientists suspect that it could have more moons that we do not know of.

Saturn

Saturn is the sixth planet from the Sun. It is the second biggest planet in our solar system. Saturn takes about 30 Earth years to complete one orbit around the Sun. Like all other planets, it spins on its own axis, but it spins very quickly. Due to this, a day in Saturn is less than 11 hours long. As it moves very fast, its atmosphere is very windy. The heat emerging from within its core, combined with these winds, give the planet the golden-yellow bands that are visible on its surface.

Upon Jupiter's surface

As a gas giant, Jupiter does not have a rocky surface like the terrestrial planets. However, scientists now believe that Jupiter may have a solid core that could possibly be as big as our Earth. Its surface has dense clouds that vary in colours like brown, red and yellow. Jupiter is a windy planet. Jupiter has a Great Red Spot. This is a storm that is said to be greater than Earth in size and has been spinning (showing similar characteristics to a hurricane) for many years.

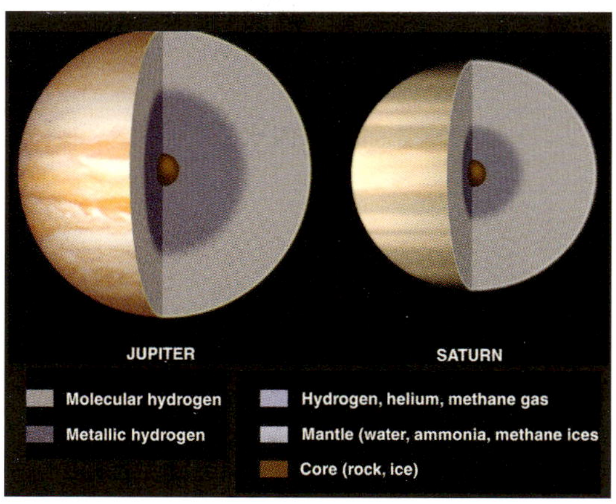

Saturn's gassy surface

Hydrogen and helium make up its surface. Layers of liquid metallic hydrogen and liquid hydrogen build up from the core. Jupiter's core is made entirely of rock, water, ice and other solid matter. Its core is made solid by the extreme heat and pressure it experiences.

FUN FACT

The atmosphere around Jupiter contains hydrogen in large portions. It also contains helium. This is very similar to the atmosphere of the Sun. If Jupiter were 80 times larger, it would have been a star just like the Sun.

Saturn's moons

Saturn has 53 known moons. Scientists have discovered nine more bodies around Saturn that could be its moons. They are called "provisional moons" and are under observation. They are being studied to confirm the same. Saturn's moons look very different from each other with regards to size, shape and appearance. They also vary in age. The moons closer to Saturn's surface have icy surfaces and hard crusts.

Incredible Ice Giants

Uranus and Neptune are the last two planets of the solar system. Earlier, it was believed that Pluto, which is located after Neptune, was a planet. Now we know that it is a dwarf planet and not a real planet.

Uranus

Uranus is the seventh planet of our solar system. One year on Uranus is the same as 84 Earth years. Uranus and Neptune are known as ice giants. Like Jupiter and Saturn, the atmosphere of Uranus is also made of hydrogen and helium. Its atmosphere contains some amounts of methane, which gives Uranus its bluish-green colour. It has 13 rings surrounding it.

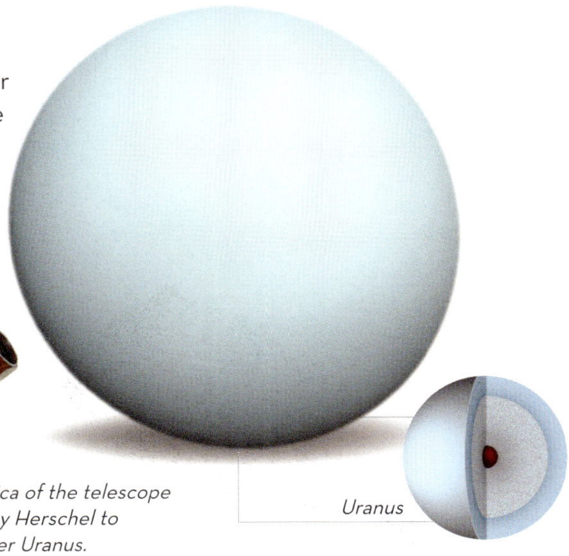

A replica of the telescope used by Herschel to discover Uranus.

Summer lasts for 20 years on Uranus.

Uranus has seasons that last up to 20 Earth years. This is because it appears to rotate on its side. This is unlike other planets that spin on their axis like a top. As Uranus rotates on its axis, it resembles a barrel that is rolling on its sides. This is because of Uranus' unusual tilt. It is possible that Uranus' axis has been tilted this way due to a collision with a large body that might have been as big as Venus. This collision may have occurred sometime after it was formed.

Uranus was discovered by accident.

In 1781, William Herschel discovered Uranus while looking at the sky with his self-created telescope along with his sister. He and his sister first believed it to be a comet.

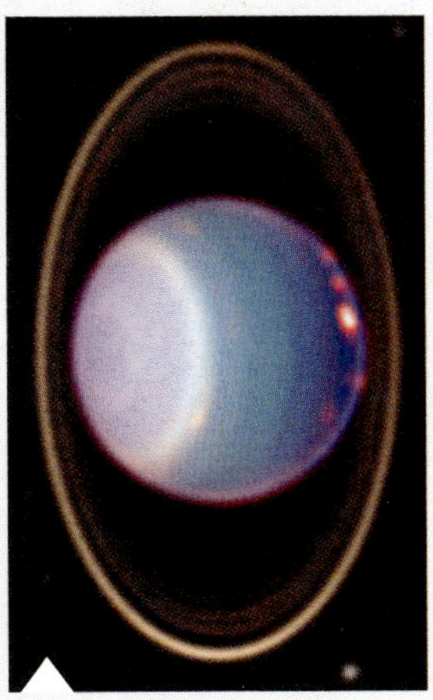

A photo of Uranus with its rings, cloud bands and moons taken by the Hubble Space Telescope.

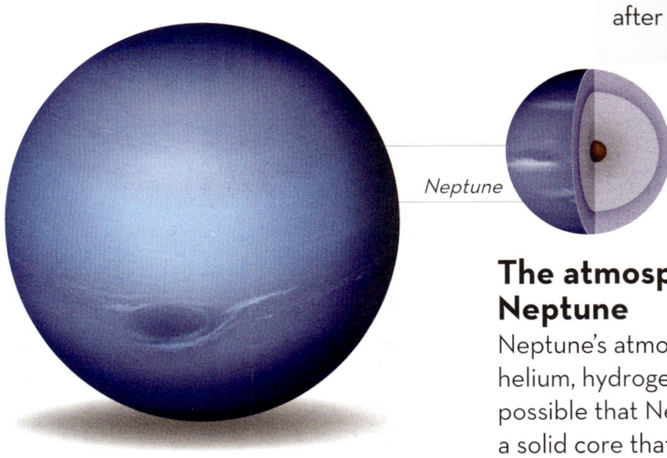

Neptune

Neptune is the eighth planet from the Sun. As it is so far away from the Sun, it takes Neptune about 165 Earth years to complete one orbit around the Sun. How many orbits do you think Neptune has completed since its discovery in 1846? Only one. This was back in 2011! A day in Neptune is 16 hours long.

The atmosphere on Neptune

Neptune's atmosphere is composed of helium, hydrogen and methane gas. It is possible that Neptune, like Jupiter, has a solid core that is as big as, or greater in size than, our Earth. Scientists have been able to confirm that Neptune has 13 moons and are looking into another body that could possibly be a moon.

Neptune is named after the Roman god of the sea.

OTHER CELESTIAL BODIES

The Oort Cloud is named for Jan Oort, who put forth the theory that a large percentage of comets are originally from a shell-like structure which surrounds the solar system. This structure is made entirely of more than a trillion large, different-sized icy bodies known as comets.

Comets

Comets are balls of ice and dust in orbit around the Sun. We can often see comets from Earth when they get close to the Sun, because the Sun's heat vaporises material from their surface, and this vapour forms a tail. A comet's orbit may take it very close to the Sun and then far away again. Comets are classified based on their orbital periods or the time they take to revolve round the Sun. Long-period comets are those that take more than 200 years to complete one orbit around the Sun. They are believed to originate from the Oort Cloud.

Comets that take nearly 200 Earth years or less to complete one orbit around the Sun are called short-period comets. Halley's Comet is a short-period comet. We can see this comet from Earth every 75–76 years. Short-period comets come from the Kuiper Belt.

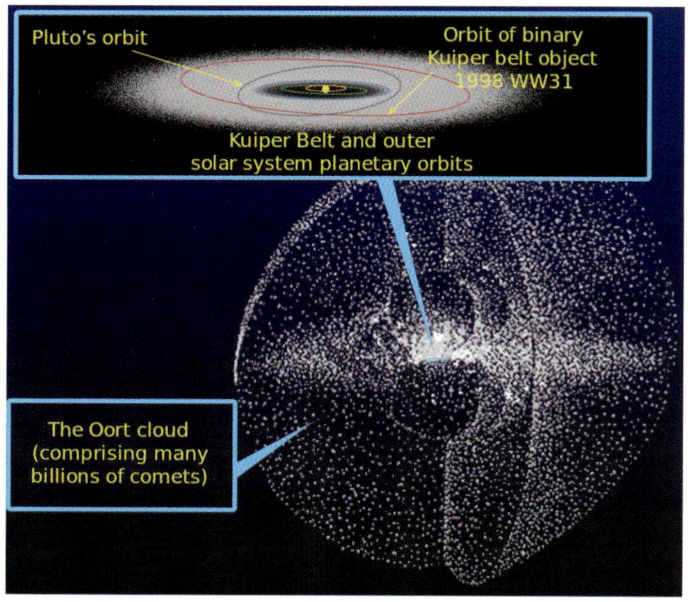

The Kuiper Belt

The Kuiper Belt is a disc-shaped region of icy bodies - including the dwarf planets. The Kuiper Belt lies beyond Neptune's orbit, just before Pluto and has a doughnut-shaped, ring-like structure.

The Halley's Comet will next appear in the year 2061.

Scientists are greatly interested in the Kuiper Belt, the Oort Cloud and their contents as the comets and other bodies within them are proposed to be remains from the formation of the solar system. They could possibly contain answers to many perplexing questions about the origin of the solar system.

The Hoba meteorite in Namibia.

Meteoroids, meteors and meteorites

Small pieces of stony or metallic debris traveling in outer space are called meteors. They sometimes fall into the atmosphere of a planet (such as Earth) as shooting stars as this encounter with the atmosphere of a planet leaves a line of light in the sky. The meteors that reach the surface of a planet are called "meteorites".

Asteroids

The Main Belt, which lies between Mars and Jupiter, consists of billions of pieces that orbit our Sun. Scientists believe that these pieces were unable to merge with others to form the planets in this area. They are also unable to come together as one object because of Jupiter's strong gravity. These pieces are called asteroids. There are some asteroids at the exterior of this belt that travel along Jupiter's orbit. They are called "Trojans" after the Greek legend.

Asteroids.

MARVELLOUS MOON

The moon is Earth's only natural satellite. Some of the matter which formed Earth has also formed the moon. The moon is nearly one-fourth of Earth's size. Like Earth, it has a rocky surface made entirely of solid matter. The surface of the moon, as is visible from Earth, has many craters. While all planets orbit the Sun, the moon orbits Earth. The moon takes 27 Earth days to complete one orbit around Earth.

Astronauts have brought back rocks from the moon.

FUN FACT

It is said that Earth was hit by large chunks of hard rocks and icy substances. One such chunk must have hit Earth too hard, causing a part of it to break away. This part became the moon.

The lunar cycle

The moon takes roughly the same amount of time to complete one rotation as it does to complete one orbit around Earth. Due to this, the Sun's light falls on different parts of the moon during different times of its rotation. So, we can see different shapes of the moon.

Does the moon cause tides on Earth?

Yes. The Sun and the moon's gravity exert influence or "pull" the water on Earth's surface, causing tides. The intensity, duration, height and timing of each tide changes according to the moon's position in the sky. Tides are at their highest during a full moon night.

The "dark side" of the moon!

Like Earth, the moon also spins on its own axis. Due to this, we see the same side of the moon while it is orbiting Earth. The side of the moon we cannot see is called "the dark side of the moon". However it is not really dark as the name suggests. If the moon remained stationary, we would be able to see the other side of the moon and clearly learn for ourselves that the moon follows a day-night cycle like Earth. The other side of the moon is not dark. It is only experiencing night.

Moon with its phases and rotation cycle.

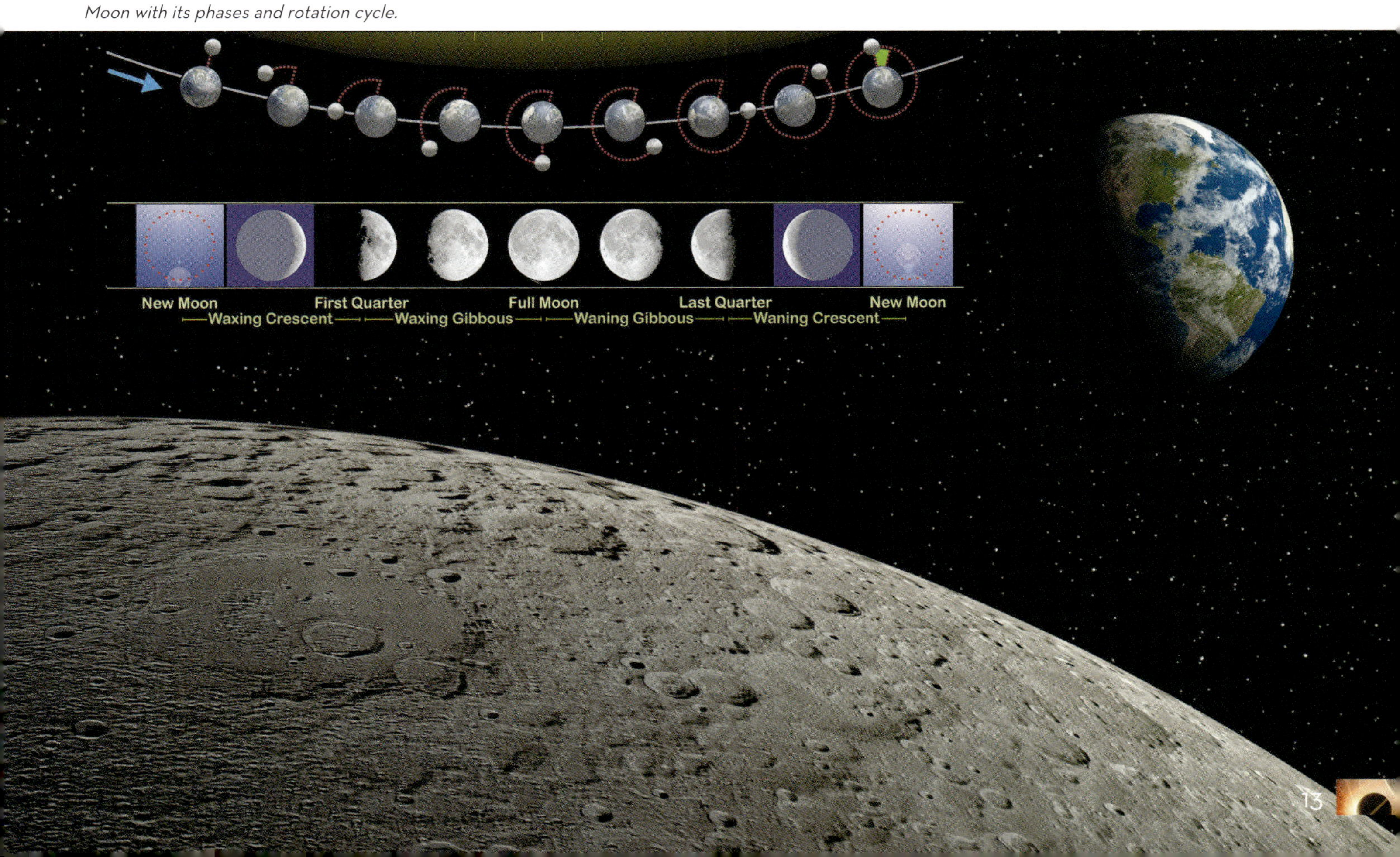

UNDERSTANDING ECLIPSES

We experience an eclipse when the moon, Earth and Sun fall in one line, causing one of these bodies to block the Sun's light from another. Based on the positions of the Sun, the moon and Earth at this time, we say it is a solar eclipse or a lunar eclipse.

How does it work?

The Sun is much larger than Earth, and Earth is much larger than the moon, so how is the moon blocking the Sun's light from Earth?

Remember that the moon is closer to Earth than the Sun. This is why the Sun and moon appear more or less the same size to us when we see them in the sky. Due to the proximity of the moon and the distance of the Sun, when the moon comes between the Sun and Earth, the Sun's light gets blocked, even though they are so drastically different in sizes.

Solar eclipse

For the duration of a solar eclipse, the moon is aligned between the Sun and Earth; thus, blocking out the rays of light in Earth's line. A solar eclipse lasts for less than eight minutes. For every century, Earth experiences about 66–75 solar eclipses. These are spread out across the years. So, one year could have one, two or three solar eclipses, or none at all. There were five solar eclipses during the year 1935. But this rare phenomenon may not occur again until 2206.

During a solar eclipse, we can see different forms of the Sun depending upon where we are standing on Earth. If you are standing outside the moon's shadow, you will see that the Sun is only partially covered by the moon. If the moon's shadow falls in the region you are standing, you will see a total eclipse, that is, the Sun is completely blocked by the moon.

Total solar eclipse

For the duration of a total solar eclipse, the moon completely covers the Sun, and hence Earth does not receive any direct rays from the Sun.

Is it safe to view a solar eclipse?

No. Have you been told to avoid looking at the Sun for a long time? This is because the solar radiations that reach Earth's surface can harm the retina of your eyes. Viewing the solar eclipse can burn portions of the retina and cause a problem known as "eclipse blindness". We can view the solar eclipse using protective eyewear made of solar lenses.

Sometimes, a smaller moon is seen covering the Sun.

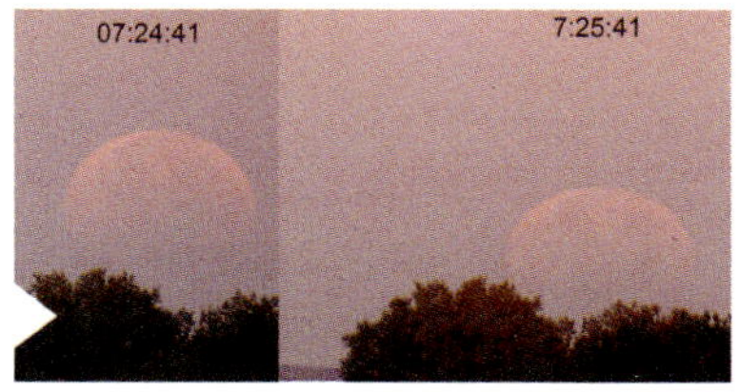

Photos of a lunar eclipse viewed from Minneapolis, Minnesota, in October 2014 with a partially eclipsed moon still up after sunrise.

FUN FACT

The website for National Aeronautics and Space Administration (NASA) gives a schedule of the lunar and solar eclipses in a year.

Lunar eclipse

During a lunar eclipse, Earth is aligned between the Sun and the moon; thus, blocking out the rays of light in the moon's line. If we look at the moon at a point during the lunar eclipse when the Sun's light is completely blocked by Earth, we would think that it looks darker than usual.

We experience two lunar eclipses in a year. Earth casts a large shadow on the moon, and as the moon moves within the shadow, it gains a reddish appearance. This is because the sunlight in Earth's atmosphere looks scattered.

A total lunar eclipse lasts for a little less than an hour. The number of lunar eclipses within a year range from 0–3. Of these, the partial eclipses exceed the total eclipses by 7 to 6.

Types of lunar eclipses

There are three types of lunar eclipses we can see on Earth:

- **Penumbral lunar eclipse:** During the penumbral lunar eclipse, the moon is positioned within Earth's penumbra or outer shadow. The penumbral lunar eclipse is very difficult to see. Lots of planning and patience are required to catch it in the sky.
- **Partial lunar eclipse:** Once the moon enters Earth's umbra, the partial eclipse phase begins. Sometimes, the Sun, the moon and Earth are not perfectly aligned. This is called a "partial eclipse". We experience a partial eclipse before a total eclipse.
- **Total eclipse:** When the moon is completely covered by the shadow formed by Earth's alignment with it, it is called a total eclipse. During such an eclipse, the moon might appear to be a deep red colour or it might not be easily visible at all. From the moon, you could see Earth as a large disc covering the Sun and thus, blocking its light. There would be a bright light coming from the circumference of Earth, which is the only light received by the moon during this time.

ARTIFICIAL SATELLITES

An artificial satellite is built by humans. Just like the moon, an artificial satellite orbits Earth. Hence, it is called a "satellite". Some artificial satellites orbit Earth permanently and some are sent to orbit for a short time. They are manned or unmanned and all monitored by space organisations on Earth.

An artificial satellite orbiting Earth.

Who thought of sending something to space?

Sir Isaac Newton had proposed that if we launch a cannonball from the top of a mountain, keeping in mind the correct velocity and direction, it could circle Earth and finally drop. Based on his theories and research, other scholars began to find a way to send a body to space. Almost 300 years after his theory, we launched the first artificial satellite into space.

Sputnik 1

Sputnik 1 is the first artificial satellite launched by humans into space. It was sent to space on 4th October, 1957. Sputnik is in fact a name given to a series of 10 satellites that were launched into space by the Soviet Union. Sputnik 1 completed one orbit around Earth in 1 hour and 36 minutes. In order to have elliptical orbits, a satellite must move even faster than Earth or moon. Sputnik 1 was active until 1958. It was later burnt and destroyed due to Earth's atmosphere.

A replica of Sputnik 1.

Sputnik 2

Sputnik 2, launched in November 1957, was the first artificial satellite to carry a living creature—a dog named Laika—into space. It, too, orbited Earth. An artificial satellite must move about 10 times faster than Earth in order to achieve the required speed and complete an orbit.

The next Sputnik satellites launched into space sent living creatures to test the life-support equipment in a spacecraft, collect data and carry out research on the magnetic fields, temperature and pressure in those regions of outer space.

A model of Sputnik 2, which is on display at the Polytechnic Museum in Moscow.

Space is getting crowded!

Since 1957, we have launched more than 5,000 artificial satellites into space. They have different sizes and orbits, and have been launched to fulfil different functions. Most satellites are sent to collect data. Depending on their purpose, they are called weather satellites, navigation satellites, television satellites and so on.

A serious problem that we face today is space traffic. It is difficult to send more satellites into space as there are many orbiting Earth. There are great risks of them colliding with each other. They could also collide with a spacecraft during its launch, descent or even while it is still in orbit. A lot of space junk has been created from past collisions.

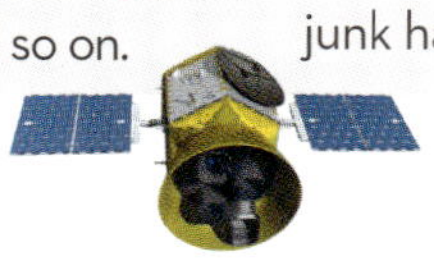

TERRIFIC TERRESTRIAL PLANETS

The first four planets closest to the Sun are Mercury, Venus, Earth and Mars. They are made up of substances like rocks, iron and other solid minerals. Hence, they are known as "inner planets" or "terrestrial planets".

Mercury

Mercury is the closest planet to the Sun. It is the smallest planet in our solar system. It has a fast spin and only takes 88 Earth days to complete one rotation around the Sun. Its surface is dry and barren. It has many craters on its surface that have been formed due to its collisions with comets and asteroids. It cannot prevent these collisions, as it does not have an adequately strong atmosphere to do so. Though other planets also have such craters, with the passage of time, these craters are reduced or erased because of their healing atmospheres, which Mercury lacks.

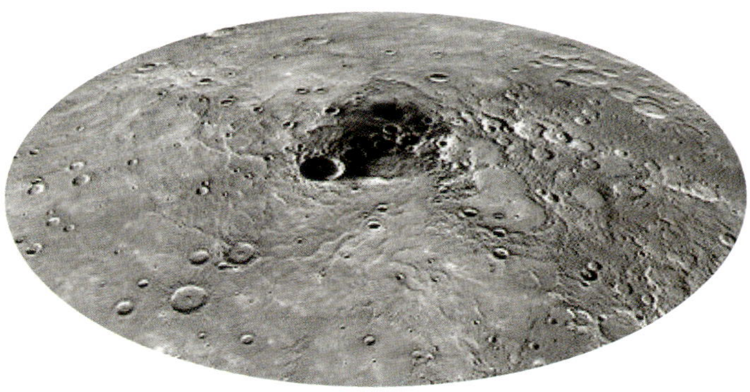

A photo showing the craters on Mercury's surface.

What is Mercury's atmosphere like?

A planet requires a strong gravity and magnetic field (among other things) to hold onto and control its atmosphere. There is very little gravity on Mercury. It has just 1 per cent of the magnetic field calculated on Earth. Hence, its atmosphere is easily blown away by stronger solar winds. If Mercury had a strong atmosphere, it could have avoided the collisions that caused its craters.

Temperature on Mercury

Due to its proximity to the Sun, Mercury experiences very high temperatures during the day. The temperature can get as high as 427 °C during the day. The temperature at night can get as low as -179 °C. This is because the side experiencing night is facing away from the Sun. The atmosphere on Mercury is so thin that it cannot control these extreme changes in temperature.

Venus

Venus is named after the Roman goddess of beauty.

Venus is the second closest planet to the Sun. It is also called "Earth's twin" or "Earth's sister planet" as its structure and size are almost the same (Venus is slightly smaller). It takes Venus 225 Earth days to complete one orbit around the Sun. However, it takes 243 Earth days to complete one rotation.

It appears to have a white-coloured surface. Sometimes, its surface also appears red due to the effect of sunlight. Its surface is covered with rocks that are grey and has many craters, and about 10,000 volcanoes.

Can we live on Venus?

No. Unlike Mercury, Venus has a very poisonous and dense atmosphere. Its proximity to the Sun also contributes to it being the hottest planet in our solar system. The temperature at its surface can get as high as 471 °C. Due to these reasons, we cannot live on Venus.

EARTH AND ITS NEIGHBOUR

Earth and Mars are the next two terrestrial planets of the solar system. As they are terrestrial planets, they have rocky surfaces and hard cores. While Earth is our home, it is said that Mars can one day become the second home to human beings.

Earth

Earth is the third planet from the Sun. It is the only planet that has life. This includes humans, trees, birds and insects. The time taken by Earth to complete one rotation (or complete one spin on its own axis) is calculated as 24 hours or one day. We experience seasons like winter and summer because of Earth's rotation. This is also why we experience day and night. It takes 365 days, or one year, for Earth to complete one orbit around the Sun.

Mars, Earth and Moon.

More about Earth

Earth is the largest terrestrial planet and the only planet which has 70 per cent of its surface covered by water. Though other planets also have atmospheres, only Earth has a "breathable" atmosphere, which means that we can only breathe life-supporting air on Earth. The atmosphere protects Earth from collisions with meteorites. If a meteorite were to enter Earth's atmosphere, it would break into many small pieces.

FUN FACT

Mars has a surface gravity of 37 per cent. What does this mean? Imagine that your friend is standing on Earth and you are standing on Mars. You both jump with the same amount of energy. You will be able to jump three times higher because of Mars' surface gravity!

Earth's natural satellite

The moon is Earth's natural satellite. Earth and moon were formed around the same time, nearly 40 million years after our solar system was formed. The moon causes high and low tides in the water on Earth.

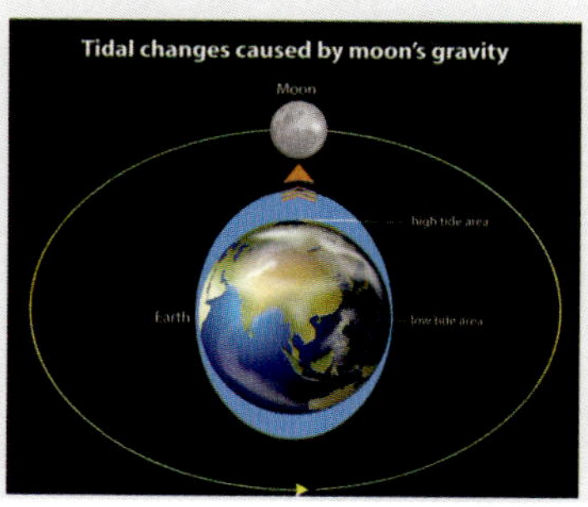

Mars

Mars is the fourth planet from the Sun. It is also called the "red planet" as the soil on Mars has a high content of iron. Over time, this iron has rusted and turned red. The dust clouds that move upwards from the soil give the sky on Mars a reddish appearance.

It takes Mars roughly two Earth years to complete one orbit around the Sun. A day on Mars is just slightly longer than a day on Earth. Mars has two moons named "Phobos" and "Deimos".

Deimos

Phobos

Water on Mars

Mars is considered a future home to human beings because we have found water on its surface. However, the atmosphere on Mars is very thin. Here, water does not remain as a liquid for a very long time. Instead, we can find ice water in extremely cold regions and salty water in other regions.

CURIOUS CONTINENTS

Earth's surface is covered with large stretches of land and water. There is no set pattern to the way land and water is divided on Earth's surface. A large, continuous landmass is called a "continent". The land on Earth is divided into seven continents. These are Asia, Africa, North America, South America, Antarctica, Europe and Oceania (in order of size).

In 1915, German geophysicist Alfred Wegener published *The Origin of Continents and Oceans*, a book about his theory on the beginning of continents. He believed that 300 million years ago, Earth's land was joined together as one large supercontinent named "Pangaea". It was surrounded by one large, continuous stretch of ocean named "Panthalassa". Over millions and millions of years, this supercontinent slowly broke apart and wafted away to form the seven continents of today. This is called "continental drift".

CONTINENTAL DRIFT

The concept of continental drift was first explored by Alfred Wegener in the early 1900s. He used this phenomenon to explain the formation of the seven continents. Fossils collected from the continents showed certain similarities. Even today, we can see that animals, plants and rock formations from two different continents share certain similarities. This sparked curiosity amongst people. This curiosity was the reason behind the continental drift theory.

What is continental drift?

Continental drift is one of the first theories that provided an explanation as to why parts of the supercontinent broke apart and moved. According to the theory, sometime in the past, landmasses from the supercontinent "drifted" away from each other. These landmasses moved Earth's mantle. Some of these landmasses also clashed into each other.

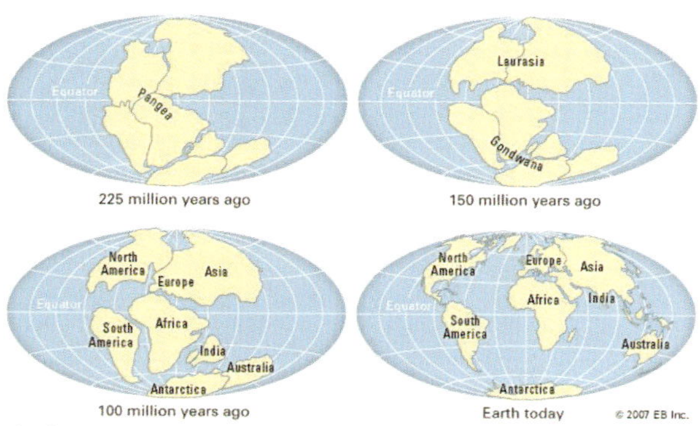

The four major phases of the continental drift theory.

When did Pangaea begin to break apart?

According to Wegener, Pangaea began to break into fragments about 200 million years ago. These fragments slowly moved away and settled into their current positions. The landmasses of North America and South America drifted towards the west while Antarctica drifted towards the South Pole. The landmass that of India drifted eastwards, then collided and merged with Asia. In 1937, a geologist named Alexander L. Du Toit further enhanced Wegener's theory. He proposed that Pangaea first split into Laurasia in the Northern Hemisphere and Gondwana in the Southern Hemisphere.

Pangaea.

Supporting theories

The credit for the continental drift theory goes to Alfred Wegener. However, some geographers in the past have made observations similar to this theory. In the 1800s, Alexander von Humboldt suggested that South America and Africa must have been joined together at some point. He based this observation on the fact that their boundaries were facing each other. The African boundary has a curved bulge that fits well with the eastern boundary of South America, making them look like two pieces of the same puzzle.

In the 1850s, Antonio Snider-Pellegrini, a French scientist, supported the idea that South America and Africa were once joined. He believed that their separation opened up the Atlantic Ocean. He observed that the fossil plants found in parts of Australia are similar to those found in South America. As fossils are found from coal deposits, it is possible that the continents were connected. Otherwise, there wouldn't be such a strong fossil similarity.

Alfred Wegener.

Laurasia and Gondwana

The first mention of Laurasia and Gondwana was made by Alexander Du Toit in *Our Wandering Continents*. According to the theory, Laurasia further fragmented to include the continents of North America, Europe and Asia (without India). Gondwana in the Southern Hemisphere further fragmented into South America, Africa and Australia and also the smaller landmasses of Arabia, India and Madagascar, which later joined with other continents. Laurasia and Gondwana were separated by an ocean named "Tethys".

Laurasia, Gondwana and the Tethys ocean.

FUN FACT

According to research, it is believed that two other supercontinents, Pannotia and Rodinia, which existed before Pangaea billions of years ago, also underwent the fragmentation of continents like Pangaea.

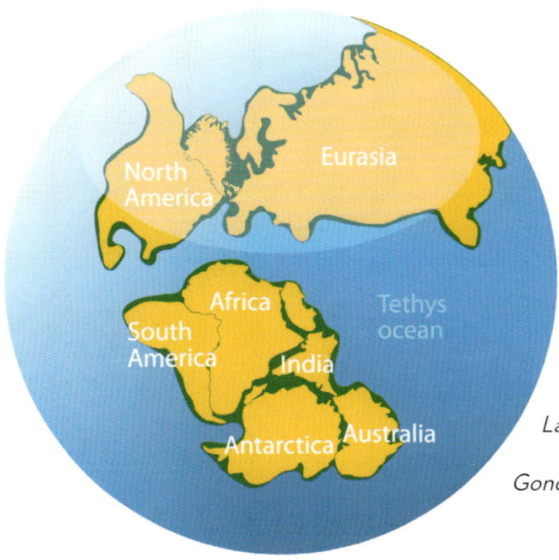

Laurasia and Gondwana.

Modern world.

The Himalayas

According to a theory by Alexander Du Toit, Gondwana eventually drifted towards the part of Laurasia that had the current continents of Europe and North America. This part was called, "Euramerica". India collided with the part that contained the current continents of Europe and Asia. The Himalayas were said to have been formed due to this collision. The Himalayas were said to have been formed about 50 million years ago and are said to be one of the youngest mountain ranges in the world.

What caused continental drift?

Wagener believed that large chunks of land began breaking away from Pangaea because of tidal forces. He also believed that some continents had to move through the oceanic crust. From his observations, he calculated that the continents of Europe and North America were slowly drifting away at the speed of 250 cm per year. Due to these observations, the theory was widely unaccepted and received a lot of criticism from his peers. They believed that there could not be a tidal force strong enough to split such large masses of land. If there were such a strong tidal force, it would affect Earth's rotation severely and possibly stop Earth's rotation within a year.

Also, a collision between a continent and an oceanic crust would not leave either body unharmed and the continents would have looked much different than they do today. Due to these reasons, the continental drift theory was rejected and replaced by the plate tectonics theory much later.

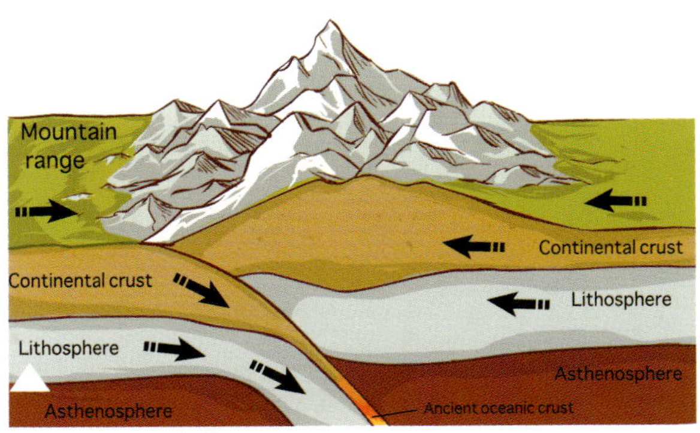

Two continental plates converge.

THE PLATE TECTONICS THEORY

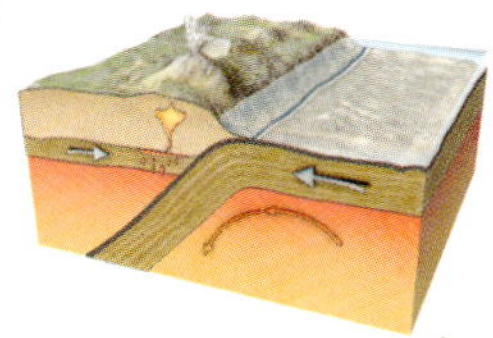

Plate tectonics is considered to be one of the most important theories of geography. This theory was developed from Alfred Wegener's continental drift theory. The word "tectonics" originated from the Greek word "tektonikos", which translates to "related to construction". This theory was developed and improved by several geophysicists from Canada, the United Kingdom and America.

What is it about?

The plate tectonics theory states that the lithosphere has been divided into fifteen tectonic plates. Tectonic plates are large blocks of hard, rocky land. Tectonic plates can be 100-200 km thick. Tectonic plates are composed of hard rocks from Earth's crust and the hard upper part of the mantle (lithosphere). These tectonic plates move upon the asthenosphere in a manner similar to the movement of ice breakers in a body of water.

Why do tectonic plates move?

As we know, the raging heat of the core escapes into the asthenosphere and the magma rises upwards. Here, it slowly cools, causing the rocks in the mantle to "flow". This forces the tectonic plates above to move.

Convergence

When two oceanic plates collide, one plate slips beneath the other. When an oceanic plate collides with a continental plate, the oceanic plate slips beneath the continental plate as it is heavier. However, when two continental plates collide, neither of them can be subducted. Instead they react with each other to form mountains.

Terminology

Tectonic plates of the continental crust are called "continental plates". These are mostly made of granite. Tectonic plates of the oceanic crust are called "oceanic plates" and are mostly made of the heavier basalt.

Collision

The movement of tectonic plates often leads to collisions. These collisions are very slow and take place when two tectonic plates come together or "converge". Based on the types of plates that are converging, when two plates collide, one of the plates might be forced below the other through the process of subduction. This results in the formation of new matter in the tectonic plate. The subducted plate is forced lower and might be pushed down to a depth of 300-700 km. At this depth, the subducted plate enters the mantle, causing some parts of it to melt.

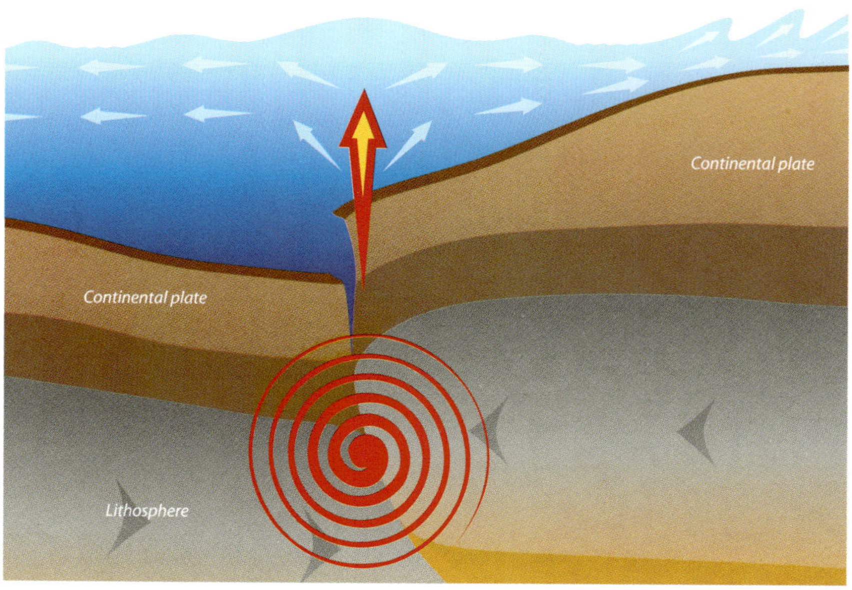

Divergence

When two plates move away from each other or "diverge", a process called seafloor spreading takes place. When two tectonic plates diverge, the magma and basalt from the mantle rise upwards. Seawater causes the hot magma to cool. This causes the formation of a new oceanic crust. Seafloor spreading usually takes place at places where mountain ranges rise from the floor of the ocean. The new oceanic crust pushes the old matter lower and, just as we see in the process of converging plates, the subducted matter melts in the magma.

The oceanic floor of the Red Sea and the Sinai Peninsula were created by the process of seafloor spreading when the African and Arabian plates diverged. It is predicted that within a few million years, Asia and North America will be separated as the plates of the Sinai Peninsula diverge.

The Red Sea and the Sinai Peninsula.

Mid-ocean ridges

Mid-ocean ridges are an extensive range of mountains. About 90 per cent of these mountain ranges lie deep in the ocean. When two oceanic plates diverge, a new oceanic plate is created. A mid-ocean ridge is formed along its boundary. This is why a mid-ocean ridge can also be called "divergent plate boundary" or "spreading centre". Tectonic plates undergo the process of diverging very slowly. They move about 1 cm to 20 cm apart every year. The mid-ocean ridge is spread 65,000 km across Earth.

Can we see mid-ocean ridges from land?

Yes, but we can only the crest. The top of the mid-ocean ridge is called "crest". Usually, a mid-ocean ridge is at the depth of 2,500 m from sea level. However, some crests rise above the sea level and are visible to us. An example of this is the Reykjanes Ridge in Iceland.

Reykjanes Ridge, Iceland.

FUN FACT

Though people believe the opposite, it is true that the ocean is deeper as we move towards the continents and away from the mid-ocean ridges.

The recycling seafloor

The process of seafloor spreading is continuous and each step in the process is important for the next step to take place. As the tectonic plates diverge, the magma rises up and forms the new seafloor. The magma that rises upwards also forces the formation of igneous rocks in the mid-ocean ridges. It is due to this process that mid-ocean ridges slowly diverge further.

The opposite ends of the mid-ocean ridge are forced apart by the process of seafloor spreading. This makes room for the formation of new seafloor and igneous rocks. Just like the new continental crust, a new seafloor is also formed continuously, ensuring the shape and size of Earth remains the same. The only way this process can stop is if the mid-ocean ridge of an area gets subducted.

A diagram showing the formation of mid-ocean ridges.

CONTINENTS:  ASIA AND AFRICA

The seven continents have great dissimilarities between them. They vary in size, composition, physical features and climatic features. Landmasses are classified as continents based on the older and younger geologically active areas. Except Antarctica, all continents are wider at the north and tapered towards the south. So, they are described as "wedge-shaped" continents.

Asia: coordinates and neighbours

Coordinates: 46.2830° N, 86.6700° E

Area: 44,579,000 km^2 (largest continent by size)

The name "Asia" is derived from the Assyrian word "Asu" meaning "east".

Neighbours: Asia's neighbours are North America in the northeast, Europe in the west and Australia in the southeast. Asia has the Arctic Ocean to its north, the Pacific Ocean to its east and the Indian Ocean to its south. To its southwest are the Mediterranean and Black Sea.

Asia: population

Population: 4.427 billion (as of 2014)
Countries: 48
Largest country: China
Smallest country: Maldives

Asia is composed of four-fifths of the Eurasian plate and a large portion of the Asian plate. Due to its large size, Asia varies in climate, physical features, wildlife and vegetation as we go from the north to the south.

The people in Asia are also very different from each other in terms of appearance, culture and lifestyle. China and India, two of the most populated countries in the world, are a part of Asia. Russia and Turkey are a part of the Asian continent, but some parts of these countries fall under the European continent.

FUN FACT

Ancient Greeks believed that as Earth is round, there must be a landmass to the south of the globe as there is to the north. They named this theoretical landmass "Antarctica", which means "opposite to the Arctic".

Africa: coordinates and neighbours

Caption: A map of Africa
Coordinates: 7.1881° N, 21.0936° E
Area: 30,221,532 km^2 (second-largest continent by size)
Neighbours: The equator divides Africa into two unequal halves. Most of Africa enjoys a tropical climate. Africa has the Atlantic Ocean to the west, the Mediterranean Sea to the north, and the Red Sea and Indian Ocean to the east. The waters of the Atlantic Ocean and Indian Ocean come together towards the south of Africa.

The "dark continent"

In the past, Africa was called the "dark continent" because the world knew very little about it. Today, we are well-informed of the happenings in Africa.

More about Africa

Population: 4.427 billion (as of 2014)
Countries: 54
Largest country: Algeria
Smallest country: Seychelles

Africa makes up one-fifth of Earth's total landmass. It is an underdeveloped continent despite being rich in various resources. Only a few countries in South and North Africa have been able to grow economically. A major portion of Africa's population is involved in agriculture.

People of Africa.

CONTINENTS:  NORTH AMERICA AND SOUTH AMERICA

North America and South America are together called the "Americas". They lie entirely within the western hemisphere. It was earlier named "America" after an Italian explorer named Amerigo Vespucci. He conducted many voyages to South America and wrote about them in letters to his friends back in Italy.

North America: coordinates and neighbours

Coordinates: 48.1667° N, 100.1667° W

Area: 24,709,000 km² (third-largest continent by size)

Neighbours: North America starts out at the Arctic Circle and stretches a little below the Tropic of Cancer. North America has the Arctic Ocean to its north, the Atlantic Ocean to its east and the Caribbean Sea to its south. The North Pacific Ocean lies to the west of North America. North America is only connected by land to South America (via the Isthmus of Panama). It is separated by its neighbours.

North America: population

Population: approximately 565 million (as of 2014)

Countries: 23 (with 22 territories and dependencies)

Largest country: Canada

Smallest country: St Kitts and Nevis (a two-island country in the Caribbean)

Most of North America's population comprises immigrants from Europe and Africa. Besides these, the first people to enter North America, also called the "original inhabitants" before the entry of the Europeans and Africans, were a group of different tribes referred to as "Native Americans" or "American Indians".

A Native American of the past.

Economically, North America is a developed continent with varied resources. North America is industrially advanced. It produces a large share of the world's oil and coal, and also generates a lot of electrical power.

South America: coordinates and neighbours

Coordinates: 13.0000° S, 59.4000° W

Area: 17,840,000 km² (fourth-largest continent by size)

Neighbours: To the north and northwest of South America is the Caribbean Sea. The Atlantic Ocean bounds the east, southeast and northeast of South America, while the Pacific Ocean bounds the west. Drake Passage, at the southern tip of Cape Horn, divides South America and Antarctica. South America makes up one-eighth of the total landmass on Earth.

South America: population

Population: approximately 387 million (as of 2014)

Countries: 12 (French Guiana and Falkland Islands are French and British territories respectively)

Largest country: Brazil

Smallest country: Suriname (a sovereign state)

South America has a diverse population consisting mainly of people from Africa and other Latin countries. This population is a result of mixing four generations of immigrants (people that originally belong to other countries but have now settled here). Most of South America is economically underdeveloped. The rural areas are mainly into agriculture while only some cities are industrially inclined.

Map of North and South America.

CONTINENTS:  ANTARCTICA, EUROPE AND AUSTRALIA

With its freezing temperatures, Antarctica is known for being the coldest, driest and windiest among all continents. Europe shares a border with Asia, while being surrounded by two oceans and three seas as well. Australia, often called "The land down under", is surrounded by two oceans – the Pacific Ocean and the Indian Ocean.

Antarctica: coordinates and neighbours

Coordinates: 90.0000° S, 0.0000° W
Area: 14,000,000 km² (fifth-largest continent by size)
Neighbours: Antarctica lies at the southernmost point of the world. It is almost circular in shape, except for the Antarctic Peninsula, which flares out towards the south of the South American continent.

Who lives in Antarctica?

Antarctica has zero "permanent population", which means that so far, no one has settled forever in Antarctica. However, every year, about 4,000 scientists visit Antarctica to carry out research and find information. A small number of people visit Antarctica for tourism.

Antarctica is always covered in snow. This is why it is called the "white continent". On the hottest day, Antarctica's temperature ranges from -15° C to -35° C, while on the coldest day, it ranges from -40° C to -70° C (these are freezing temperatures!), so it is unsafe to live here. Antarctica is also called the "freezing continent" because of its frigid temperatures. Antarctica experiences the strongest winds. Only certain plants, algae, lichens and some animal species have been able to adapt themselves to live in Antarctica.

Europe: coordinates and neighbours

Coordinates: 54.9000° N, 25.3167° E
Area: 10,180,000 km² (sixth-largest continent)
Neighbours: Europe is composed of the western portion of the Eurasian plate. It makes up for one-fifteenth of the world's landmass. It has the Arctic Ocean to its north and the Atlantic Ocean to its south. The Kuma-Manych Depression, the Black Sea, the Caspian Sea and the Mediterranean Sea bound the southern point of Europe. The east and southeast of Europe is bordered by the continent of Asia.

Europe: population

Population: 738.44 million (as of 2015)
Countries: 51
Largest country: Russia
Smallest country: Vatican City (an independent microstate)
Each country of Europe speaks a different language. The countries have connected but majorly different heritages that have given way to largely different cultures and practices. The population of Europe also includes immigrants from Asia and Africa, however, these are still lesser than the original inhabitants.

Australia: coordinates and population

Coordinates: 35.3080° S, 149.1245° E
Area: 7,692,024 km² (smallest continent)
Countries: 1 (Australia)
Capital: Canberra
Population: 23.97 million (as of 2015)
Neighbours: Australia has just one country. This is why it is alternately referred to as a continent and also a country. As a country, it is one of the largest in the world. Australia lies entirely in the Southern and Eastern Hemisphere and is bordered by the Pacific Ocean and the Indian Ocean. The island of Tasmania to the southern tip of Australia is separated from the mainland by the Bass Strait.

Sydney, Australia.

NATURE'S WONDERS

The shaking, moving, crumpling, crunching and spinning land and water sometimes work together to form unbelievably beautiful structures. From deep blue waters with hidden treasures, to phenomenal islands with pretty white sand and the blinking northern lights, nature has many attractions for us to explore.

There are no efforts made by humans to create or beautify these natural wonders. However, we do take great care to maintain these structures and protect them from any causes that might destroy them. These structures have been created through reactions on Earth over a period of millions of years. Without them, Earth would not be half as magical or mysterious as it is today.

THE GREAT BARRIER REEF

The Great Barrier Reef is located on the east coast of Australia. It is one of the most breathtaking natural wonders of the world. Stretching 2000 km from northwest to southeast and covering an area of 3,50,000 km^2, it is the world's largest coral reef.

A diverse ecosystem

The Great Barrier Reef actually consists of 2,100 individual coral reefs and 800 fringing reefs. There are 400 different species of reefs located here. The latter refers to the reefs that border coastlines and islands. It is a rich and diverse ecosystem with more than 2000 species of fish, 4000 species of mollusc and 250 species of shrimp. There are about 940 islands, islets and cays here.

The Great Barrier Reef has a co-dependent ecosystem.

Coral Sea

The Coral Sea is a part of the southwestern area of the Pacific Ocean. It stretches from the east of Australia and New Guinea to the west of New Caledonia. It is named after the many coral reefs found in the Great Barrier Reef.

The Great Barrier Reef and the Coral Sea.

Formation and protection

Though the reefs of the Great Barrier Reef are of different species, they are formed from the biological wastes, skeletal wastes and remains of marine life from millions of years ago. The polyps and hydrocorals with the coralline algae and bryozoans have formed these reefs.

Great Barrier Reef was declared a World Heritage site in 1981 for being one of the most diverse places on Earth. To protect and maintain this natural wonder, the government of Australia created the Great Barrier Reef Marine Park in 1975. It is the world's largest national marine sanctuary.

Biodiversity

It is not just corals that live in the Great Barrier Reef, but also many species of aquatic life. The Great Barrier Reef Marine Park aims to protecting and helping the survival of the variety of species that live in this natural wonder.

The Whitemouth eel is one of the species that lives in the Great Barrier Reef.

There are many different species of wildlife living here. Green turtles, dugong, dolphins and whales are some examples of this wildlife.

Around 2006, there numbers of dugongs and green turtles in the reef were reducing due to habitat problems. In 2004, the Marine Park rezoned the areas as a method to identify the different habitats and species, and also the areas that need attention.

Green turtle.

Great Barrier Reef and James Cook

On 10th June, 1770, British explorer and navigator James Cook was sailing along the coast of Eastern Australia. He was travelling on HM Bark Endeavour, a British Royal Navy Research Endeavour. It struck against an outcrop.

A portrait of Captain James Cook.

Though most of the crew aboard the ship were alright, the ship itself was greatly damaged. The crew took an entire day to move it from the path of the high tide. They threw out the heavy items on the ship such as the carriages, guns, casks, stores of food and more.

After some struggle, the crew began to work on repairing the ship. Nearly a month later, on 9th July, 1770, Guugu Yimithirr (an Aboriginal tribe that lived here) men spotted them. When James Cook tried to speak to them, they ran away as him and his crew were the first Europeans they had seen. When he returned home, James Cook wrote about this place and spread word of it to Europeans.

Another explorer and cartographer, Matthew Flinders, who had many experiences with the Great Barrier Reef, later gave this natural wonder its name. He was inspired to name it this by its size and by the reefs present here.

FUN FACT

It is said that if we were to take out the main parts of the Great Barrier Reef and put them all out to dry, we would need to occupy the entire state of New Jersey. Even after doing so, we would still have some corals to spare. That's how many corals the Great Barrier Reef holds within its beautiful waters!

Hot Springs and Geysers

A hot spring is a pool of water whose temperature is higher than the surrounding air temperature. This water is actually groundwater. It is flowing from an underground water source which is heated by magma or molten rock. Groundwater seeping a kilometre or more below the surface, where the rocks have a high temperature, also creates a hot spring.

This is the Sea Hell hot spring in Beppu, Japan. It is one of the most popular tourist spots of the area.

What is a geyser?

A geyser is a special kind of hot spring caused due to a pressure build up below the Earth' surface. Because of this pressure, it erupts intermittently sending jets of water and steam upwards into the air.

A geyser in Namafjall in Iceland.

Eruptions in a geyser

Earth's surface has certain holes that have a tube-like structure. They reach into Earth's crust. The bottom end of the tube has molten rocks or magma. The tube is completely filled with water. The magma at the bottom heats this water. So, the water near the bottom is very hot and boiling. The boiling water turns into steam.

The steam pushes its way to the surface, carrying some of the water with it. The water at the surface is pushed up along with the steam. This is what we call an eruption in a geyser. Once the temperatures cool, or once all the water in the tube is pushed out, the eruption stops.

A timely process

Once the eruption stops, water slowly enters the tube again. Once again, the water at the bottom is heated causing the process to repeat. If a geyser is small, the eruption will last for less than five minutes. If it is a very big geyser, then it can take several days for the eruption to stop. In many geysers, the next eruption can be predicted. The Yellowstone National Park is the world's most famous spot for geysers and hot springs.

Coral Sea

The Yellowstone National Park was created in 1872 to preserve the thermal areas, hot springs and geysers here. It is spread across the states of Wyoming, Montana and Idaho in the USA. This park lies directly above a giant hot spot with magma rising towards the surface. It has more than 10,000 geysers and hot springs.

The Misting Ponds is a thermal area in Yellowstone National Park.

The Grand Prismatic Spring is one of the larger geysers of Yellowstone National Park.

Uluru and Kata Tjuta

Driving in the desert landform of Central Australia, one might suddenly come across one of the largest monoliths in the world. Uluru or Ayers Rock, made entirely of sandstone, stands tall and proud in the middle of the sandy plains of the Central Australian desert. It is nearly 348 m tall. From left to right, it is 9.4 km wide. This natural wonder is also rich in culture and heritage as it is home to the Anangu tribe, an aboriginal tribe.

Uluru and Kata Tjuta National Park

In 1950, this national park was created to protect the interests of the Aboriginal land and also to maintain the Uluru and Kata Tjuta monoliths here. Many parts of the land were owned by Anangu traditional owners who now cooperate with the park management to maintain the land. As this site has so much cultural and natural value, it has been declared a World Heritage Site.

This park also protects the animal life present here.

Kata Tjuta

Kata Tjuta (or the Olgas) is a group of more than 30 rocks rising from the plains surrounding this structure. These rocks are stacked close together. Between these rocks, there are deep and narrow crevices. Some rocks are stacked apart from each other and are smoother due to the erosion from wind and water. The highest of all the rocks is called Mount Olga which is around 1500 feet in height. This massive structure neighbours the Uluru. Both, Uluru and Kata Tjuta are sacred for the Anangu tribe living here.

Anangu tribe

The Anangu tribe has been living in Central Australia for the past 30,000 years. They are said to be the traditional owners of Uluru and Kata Tjuta.

In 1958, when the national park was created, the Anangu tribe were left out of its management. The tribe fought for nearly 35 years to gain recognition. Besides being their home, the Anangu tribe have many legends and myths connected to the Uluru and Kata Tjuta. Their life is based on the "Tjukurpa", which is the period of time when the world was actually being formed.

Legend of the Anangu tribe

Mount Olga is believed to be the home of a snake named Wanambi. This snake curls up into a ball and stays in the waterhole of the summit during the rainy season. In the dry seasons, the snake comes out and sits in the gorge at the bottom of Mount Olga. When angry, the snake causes hurricanes.

Not only is Uluru a sacred site for the aboriginal tribe, it is also an important Australian landmark.

AURORA BOREALIS AND AURORA AUSTRALIS

Every once in a while, during the night, nature puts on a show of lights where lights in shades of blue, white, green, yellow, pink, violet and red appear in the sky in continuously changing shapes. These lights move like a curtain in a gentle breeze. They are only experienced in the extreme poles. Light auroras are seen in the mid-latitudes but there are no auroras in the equator.

The Auroras

Auroras are named after the Roman goddess "Aurora", the goddess of dawn. Auroras occur at Earth's magnetic poles at the north and the south. Aurora borealis occurs at the North Pole and is also called the "northern lights". Aurora australis occurs at the South Pole and is also called the "southern lights".

How do the auroras occur?

Sometimes, the electrons in outer space collide with the molecules of oxygen and nitrogen in the uppermost layer of the atmosphere. The electrons actually come from Earth's own magnetosphere which controls some part of the surrounding area of outer space. These electrons share their energy with the oxygen and nitrogen molecules, thus giving them an "excited" charge. Slowly, these molecules return to their normal state. While doing so, they give out photons. This is what causes the lights. If many electrons and molecules collide, the light can become visible to the people on Earth. This is what causes the aurora displays.

Disturbances caused by the auroras

An aurora creates quite a few disturbances in the working electric or magnetic equipment. In the past, people have reported damage in electronic items and disturbances in radio signals. In addition to this, many artificial satellites experience damages during an aurora. This is mainly due to the amount of electrons that come thrashing down towards Earth's magnetic field when an aurora display takes place.

Corona

Auroras stretch from east to west and cover a long distance in the sky. Sometimes, they form multicoloured bands and rays, which can be a truly breathtaking sight. Sometimes, they form a large solitary band of light that covers the sky.

A corona is the most spectacular form of a ray. It looks like an amalgamation of several colourful rays that are bursting out of a single point in the sky. There are patches of fluffy, cloud-like rays which intermingle with the rays.

Auroras also occur in dual bands, which appear like a forked ray of light.